Microsoft SharePoint Simplified for Beginners

A Beginners Guide To Microsoft SharePoint

BONIFACE BENEDICT

Dedication

This book is dedicated to God Almighty, and to my father, Boniface, for his moral support.

Table of Contents

Introduction 1

CHAPTER ONE 2

SharePoint Overview 2

    Some Key Features of SharePoint Foundation 5

CHAPTER TWO 10

About SharePoint development tools 10

CHAPTER THREE 19

Integration options on SharePoint 19

    Events and logic integration 19

    User interface integration 20

    Data Integration 22

CHAPTER FOUR 24

How to create and set up a site 24

    How to create a site 24

    Setting up groups for the site 26

    How to modify site permissions 29

CHAPTER FIVE 37

Working with pages on SharePoint 37

    How to create a Web Parts Site Page 37

    Editing a Web Part Site Page 38

    Ways to check out a Page 40

    Changing the Layout 41

    How to add a Web Part to a Page Zone 41

    Deleting a Web Part 43

    Adding Individual Content Items 43

    Editing a Page After Initial Configuration 45

CHAPTER SIX 47

Working with documents on SharePoint library 47

    Creating a New Document in a SharePoint Document Library 47

    How to upload documents to a SharePoint Document Library 48

    How to Check Out Documents 50

    How to Check-In Documents 51

    How to Move Files into Folders 52

How to Copy Files from One Folder to Another 52

How to use File Explorer to Move or Copy Between Libraries 53

CHAPTER SEVEN 55

All SharePoint list functionality 55

    Views 56

    Lookup Fields 57

    List Data Storage 58

CHAPTER EIGHT 59

Other SharePoint features and elements 59

CHAPTER NINE 65

The SharePoint Azure Platform 65

    Cloud Computing 65

    Azure Platform Overview 66

    SharePoint Apps and Microsoft Azure 70

CHAPTER TEN 73

Other SharePoint Apps 73

CHAPTER ELEVEN 80

Sandbox Solutions 80

CHAPTER TWELVE 83

SharePoint Packaging & Deploying 83

CHAPTER THIRTEEN 87

Feature/Event Receiver 87

CHAPTER FOURTEEN 90

Server Object Model 90

Conclusion 93

Introduction

Over the years, Microsoft has continually developed programs and packages that tasks and operations easier for workers and non-workers. SharePoint is another Microsoft tool that helps to create websites and securely organize, store, access, and share information. The good thing about SharePoint is that only those whom you share your site information can have access to it. Also, the information can be accessed from any kind of device using a Web browser. The information embedded in this book is to guide you with detailed steps on how to use the Microsoft SharePoint.

After completing he guides in this book, you should be able to perform several tasks like:

- Creating a SharePoint site
- Accessing a SharePoint Site
- Managing site permissions
- Becoming familiar with the Interface, Quick Launch, Ribbon, and Top Links
- Creating and managing document libraries
- Creating and formating site pages and content
- Searching for content on your SharePoint site

CHAPTER ONE

SharePoint Overview

SharePoint is a handy platform for collaboration and content management and a central web-based portal. With SharePoint, you can organize and manage your colleagues (and even your own's) social activities, documents, data, and information. With SharePoint, you can also:

> Set up centralized password-protected space for group document sharing
> You can store download documents, store and edit them before uploading for later sharing.
> SharePoint also offers a wide range of features which makes it challenging for anyone to be well-grounded across all the workloads.

Further understanding of Microsoft SharePoint reveals that it is divided into three different areas namely: Collaboration, Interoperability, and Platform.

Collaboration

The term collaboration contains in itself a strong and deeply rooted theme for the SharePoint package. This implies that you can bring different types of people together through diverse collaborations like web content management, enterprise content management, discovering people, and their respective skills as well as social computing. In the 2013 SharePoint package, collaboration is duly managed through applications. In a similar fashion, developers can customize and extend or build their own Apps for SharePoint while they can also manage these collaborations on SharePoint.

Interoperability

SharePoint also allows users to bring collaboration together with the aid of interoperability like:

> Deploying applications to the cloud or integrating with some wide web technologies.
> Ability to build and deploy custom and secure solutions which line of business data with Office and SharePoint.
> Web-based and office document integration.

Platform

SharePoint as a platform does not only support collaboration and interoperability but also give due support to extensibility through a solid set of developer tools, a rich object model, and a growing developer community. The notion of the cloud in SharePoint is one of the key paradigm shifts as it also introduces new App models like:

> New modes of authentication through OAuth
> New ways of deploying, developing and hosting diverse SharePoint applications

> New ways of data interoperability with the aid of REST and OData.

The SharePoint types

As noted earlier, it will be hard for anyone to be an expert across all workloads on SharePoint; this can be attributed to the different versions and types that SharePoint comes with. Basically, there are three ways to use and install SharePoint and they are:

> SharePoint Foundation
> SharePoint Server
> Office 365

SharePoint Server and SharePoint foundation are tagged as SharePoint on-premise while Office 365 (the third on the above list) comes as a fully cloud-hosted model of SharePoint.

SharePoint Foundation

SharePoint foundation remains a vital solution for all organizations and firms in need of a manageable, secure, and web-based collaboration platform. SharePoint Foundation is available with all the basic features of collaboration that are embedded in the SharePoint package. For instance:

> The SharePoint foundation ships to anyone as a downloadable install, free and also represents the foundational aspects of Microsoft SharePoint.

SharePoint foundation covers a good number of features like user and team site collaboration, security, and administration as well as some other Apps like lists, document libraries, and many more. SharePoint foundation also provides a baseline set of functions and features that enables all users to easily get acquainted with both developing for SharePoint and using SharePoint.

SharePoint foundation needs some few features to upgrade if it intends to build standard communication and collaboration solutions for utilization within your organization. The basic features of the SharePoint foundation evolve around collaboration and document management.

Some Key Features of SharePoint Foundation

In addition to the benefits and amazing features embedded in the Microsoft SharePoint Foundation which makes it offer some wide range adoption by business personnels, below are some key features of the package that you might find interesting.

SharePoint Foundation has better control of any company and organization's vital business data. This is made possible with the availability of information and data management features which duly secures all that you have input

SharePoint Foundation has an effective task and document collaboration. The diverse team websites uninterrupted access to information through a central location.

When you customize and extend SharePoint Foundation, you in turn embrace the web for better collaboration.

The SharePoint Foundation package is available on all customers of the Windows Server as a free download with the aid of which implementation cost and time are vastly reduced (making up a reduction in the deployment and implementation resources).

In sum of all, SharePoint foundation is a flag bearer of the collaboration and integral content storage feature of the whole of SharePoint itself. SharePoint Foundation is the ideal version for all small organizations and teams in need of improvement in their ability to work with themselves in an easy to use, secure and collaborative workspace.

SharePoint Server

What SharePoint Server offers is a wealth of features which is extended upon the ones offered by SharePoint Foundation. SharePoint Server provides a more advanced cum richer collection of the features and functions which you can make use of for your organisation's solutions.

Some Key Features of SharePoint Server

Having stated that SharePoint Server offers advanced features of the SharePoint Foundation, below are some additional and core features of the package.

> Enterprise Services: The Enterprise services feature on SharePoint Server makes a way for users to develop their custom solutions easily and quickly with the aid of the tools available within the Office product family.
> Advanced Search: The SharePoint Server offers a search functionality and feature which allows for customized Search Results pages. You can as well configure this page with the customised search Web part feature (this feature is also available within the servers version, offering better flexibility).
> Computing and Social Networking: Social networking has become an highly sought after and expected feature set with countless solutions. Interestingly, SharePoint Server is not leaving users out on this feature.
> Web Content Management: The good news about SharePoint server is that it supports publishing and web content creation for the internet. That way, you can show the world all what you have within.
> Records Management: With SharePoint Server, there is excellent and adequate support for the management of all your contents throughout its entire circle of existence.
> Business Connectivity Services: Another important feature on SharePoint Server is the Business

Connectivity Services (BCS). This allows you to connect to some other external data sources and display your business information through user profiles, Web Parts or SharePoint lists.

Office 365

Emerging the third on the list, Office 365 stands out as a fully cloud hosted version of the SharePoint program. Office 365 is the alternative option for self hosting your own farm using your on-premises Data Center.

Some Key Features of Office 365

Noting that Office 365 stands out with certain features, it is integral to outline what makes it seem good and acceptable.

Office 365 is a great place where you can quickly and easily develop series of rich applications (both as cloud hosted apps and SharePoint hosted apps). You will also scale through the cost of maintaining an on-premises infrastructure.

The options for licensing SharePoint Online available on Office 365 are based on some factors like the amount of data you intend storing, the number of authorized users you want to add as well as the features you want to make available and many more.

On Office 365, there are series of .NET applications that you can build by utilizing the Visual Basic or C# afterward you can deploy into SharePoint as .APPs or. WSPs. There are some other light weight applications like JavaScript and HTML5 which you can also deploy.

All the features and services on Office 365 are not the same as SharePoint Foundation or SharePoint Server but it also carry with it some handy tools and development abilities.

With either of Office 365, SharePoint Server or SharePoint Foundation, developers can customize the features to suit what they really want.

CHAPTER TWO

About SharePoint development tools

This chapter will be making exposition on the diverse aspects and levels of development as regard SharePoint. Note that every level serves the end-user of the SharePoint site in diverse ways. To this effect, you can divide the SharePoint development tools into:

End-users – the people who use the platform as a platform for application

Power users – this refers to those who administer and create (sometimes they also brand) sites

Designers – these people build and brand the site for the user's experience

Developers – developers (as well known) refers to those who deploy and build apps.

Ranging from developers to other end users, a wide range of people make use of and interact with the SharePoint package as outlined in the subsequent lines.

SharePoint designer

The SharePoint Designer tool makes a lot of development tasks easy. However, many developers prefer to use a different package rather than use the SharePoint Designer as a developing tool for creating SharePoint sites.

Some important features of SharePoint Designer are —

> SharePoint Designer is very handy for creating a declarative and rule-based workflow which can be later imported in the Visual Studio for a deeper as well-rooted customization
>
> SharePoint Designer package can be utilized for a wide range of designer functions on SharePoint, this includes creating and editing pages, sites, content types, and lists.
>
> On the first launch of the SharePoint Designer, users might need to make available the URL with which you intend to use for your SharePoint site and then proceed to authenticate as an elevated user.
>
> SharePoint Designer can be downloaded and further installed from https://www.microsoft.com/en-pk/download/details.aspx?id=35491
>
> Once you open your site in the SharePoint Designer, some information and navigable options about your site comes up (information like permissions, site metadata, subsites, and more).
>
> SharePoint Designer has an inheritance of the standard SharePoint permissions.

To use the SharePoint Designer, you must first set up SharePoint Designer through Office 365 by launching your SharePoint site from there. Afterward, use the guides below.

Step 1 – Start by opening the SharePoint site.

Step 2 – Select the Office 365 Settings menu option. Then Select Settings in the left pane and then select the software in the middle pane.

Step 3 – Select Tools & add-ins in the left pane, you will see the diverse options. In the end, you will see SharePoint Designer Option, click the link.

Step 4 – Open the SharePoint Designer once installed. Click the Open Site option.

Step 5 – Specify the URL for your SharePoint site and then click Open.

Step 6 – Once the SharePoint Designer site is open, you will see that various options are available.

Step 7 – Click SharePoint Lists on the Ribbon and select Tasks from the menu.

Step 8 – A new dialog box opens. Specify the name and description and click OK.

Step 9 – To go to the same site through the portal, you will see the To-Do list present on your site.

Site settings

One of the core parts of SharePoint is the site settings. Getting acquainted and being familiar with this part of SharePoint is as important as owning the package. To get familiar with it, use the steps below.

Step 1 – To access the Site Settings page, click on User Profile present in the SharePoint Admin center. Click the option Setup My Site under My Site Settings.

On this page, you will find a good number of configurations for your new site like:

Activate features.

Change the theme of your site.

Manage permissions.

Step 2 – Some other settings options are made available in the Settings. So proceed by clicking the Settings in the left pane.

You should not forget that the basic features of the site settings page are divided into some categories. For instance, a good number of your privacy and security settings are made available in theming in Web Designer Galleries, Users and Permissions category, and many more.

Add Media files

If you want to add a Media Player to your SharePoint site, you need to first launch your SharePoint site and move through to the homepage of your site as follows.

Step 1 – On the Page tab, click the Edit menu option.

Step 2 – Select the Web Part option.

Step 3 – Select the Media and Content from Categories and then select the Media with Parts from the Parts section. Click Add.

Step 4 – Save the page, instantly you will see a new page, which contains the Media file.

Add HTML page

When editing, the experience ranges from adding images to formatting texts to adding multimedia and many more. You can as well make up a little more into the code when you embed HTML directly into your SharePoint site. This task might seem somewhat laborious, however, the guide below renders help.

Step 1 – Launch your SharePoint site and move to the home page of the site. On the Page tab, then click the Edit menu option.

Step 2 – On the INSERT tab, click the Embed Code option.

Step 3 – Add some HTML code into the code field

Step 4 – Click Insert, this will show you that the HTML snippet has been inserted

Step 5 – Click Save.

Once completed, you will see that the HTML code has been inserted in your SharePoint site

Visual Studio and Expression Blend

The Visual Studio and Expression Blend allows you to add some meaningful and beautiful contents to your SharePoint site. The Visual Studio also offers a wide range of features that helps in the development of applications in SharePoint. It will be a good option if you get yourself acquainted with the features in full details.

To start and have a look at an example of a SharePoint hosted application via Visual Studio; use the guide below.

Step 1 – Open Visual Studio and then select File then New, and then click Project option.

Step 2 – In the left pane select Templates → Visual C# → Office/SharePoint and then in the middle pane select App for SharePoint. Afterward, input the name as required in the Name field then click OK (this displays a dialog box).

Step 3 − Proceed to the SharePoint admin center and copy the SharePoint URL.

Step 4 − Paste the URL in the New App for SharePoint dialog box that is shown

Step 5 − Click Next and this will open the Connect to SharePoint dialog box where you need to log in.

Step 6 − Enter your required credentials then click the Sign in button. Once you are successfully logged in to the SharePoint site, you will see a dialog box

Step 7 − Click Finish. Once the project is created, click the AppMenifest.xml file in the Solution Explorer.

Step 8 − Click on the Permissions tab. A Scope dropdown list will be displayed.

Step 9 − In the Scope dropdown list, select Web, which is the scope of permissions that you are configuring. In the Permission drop-down list, select Read, that is the type of permission you want to configure.

Step 10 − Open the Default.aspx file then replaces it with your code.

Step 11 − Head to the Solution Explorer and right-click the project then select Publish. Click the Package the app button. This builds your SharePoint-hosted app and prepares it for you to deploy it to your SharePoint site. A folder containing .app file will pop up.

Step 12 − Move to your SharePoint online site.

Step 13 − Click Apps for SharePoint in the left pane. A new page will open.

Step 14 − Drag your files here to upload. As soon as the file is uploaded, you will see a new page

Step 15 − Click the option - Site Contents in the left pane. Click the add an app icon as displayed on your screen. Subsequently, a new page will be opened.

Step 16 − Select Your Apps → From Your Organization in the left pane; this will show you that the application is available for you to install it. Click the app.

Step 17 − Once you click the app, a dialog box will open on your working screen. Click Trust it.

Step 18 − You will see that the app is installed. Immediately the installation is complete, you can now click the app. After this, you will see a new page that contains a button, if you click the Push me to button your current date be displayed.

CHAPTER THREE

Integration options on SharePoint

This chapter will be covering the diverse integration options on SharePoint. The 2013 model of SharePoint offers a huge number of options which makes your application to deeply integrate with SharePoint as well as other systems and data. The integration options are:

Events and logic integration
User interface integration
Data integration

Events and logic integration

The most prominent and integral aspect of any application is making a UI provision for users. However, the ability of users to respond to the actions (either to interact with an application or within an application) is also very vital. Some key features of Event and Logic integration includes (but not limited to):

The SharePoint 2013 makes available am event receiver which allows diverse applications to give a response to events happening inside a SharePoint site. The SharePoint package gives users the ability to duly respond to multiple activities within the. For instance, with a button click, you can respond to activities within your SharePoint site and also respond to documents that are being checked out.

Giving response to activities within your SharePoint application is very easy and straightforward. Your code and application UI is run remotely from SharePoint and both are simply surfaced through App Pages and Parts. Due to the latter said, giving responses to an event (such as in the aspect of a button that is being clicked in your application) is absolutely connected to your application's programming framework. An instance is when your application is built with ASP.NET, this way you can catch the OnClick event for an ASP.NET button.

It is noteworthy that SharePoint does not in any way affect your access to these kinds of events. SharePoint has made available some event receivers which makes for easy responding to the events that occur within SharePoint (like a document being updated or saved).

User interface integration

In the user interface integration, there are three major integration points that are always available to all users as a part of their SharePoint application model. They are as follows:

> App Parts and Pages
> Ribbon and Action menus
> Navigation

App Parts and Pages

Apps parts and pages offer users the ability to surface their application's user interface. For users who are familiar with the older version of SharePoint (SharePoint 2010), know that Apps Parts is very similar to Web Parts. Also:

> Apps Parts are configurable and reusable windows into the SharePoint application.
> Pages are very similar to an Apps Part except for the fact that they are displayed in fuller and larger windows style.

Ribbon and Action Menus

First introduced in SharePoint 2010, Ribbon and Action Menus provide a central location for all actions that a user might want to engage in to take on documents, folders, and other data. SharePoint 2010 introduced a feature that allows developers to include custom actions for their applications using the ribbon. Also, SharePoint applications for this customization. Put together will some other standard actions, SharePoint provides enables users to includes actions and functions wherever users expect them.

The Action menu on the other hand is a context-aware menu for items in a SharePoint library or list. For instance, within a SharePoint document library, common features and functions like Check and Check In are exposed (another common term used to refer to this menu is Edit Control Block).

Navigation

Just as the name suggests, the navigation feature allows you to navigate and find your apps while also integrating with the Action and Ribbon menus. This makes it easy for users to decide and take actions in some similar locations as they will within SharePoint.

When you utilize any or all of these building blocks, you integrate your application's user interface alongside that of SharePoint's and also expose your application to its user.

Data Integration

Data remains the heart of every application and what all users intend to work with whenever they use your application. SharePoint makes available a good number of outstanding options for working with and storing data and information. These options for storing and working on data includes:

> Working with data that lives external to SharePoint.
> Manipulating and Storing data within SharePoint

Right from the first version of SharePoint, the aim has been to make the process of working with data very easy, straightforward, and simple for all users. The most simple instance of this is the concept of list data which has made users able to work and store using the tabular style data (through a well-known web interface).

A lot of people assume that using lists is analogous unlike using a table of data within a database. That being said, SharePoint applications can as well make use of these similar data storage capacity through the use of lists. If properly utilized, SharePoint can help save up some time and effort and subsequently reduce the cost of support and management of your operation.

The core data storage capabilities are:

> Lists – For storing structured data, typically like in a table.
> Libraries – For storing unstructured data, like in a file or document.

Furthermore, SharePoint gives a comprehensive set of APIs to developers. This is what they use within the applications to manipulate data and interact with information that resides in SharePoint. For most SharePoint applications, all those APIs are usually exposed inside the Client-Side Object Model (CSOM).

CHAPTER FOUR

How to create and set up a site

One of the most interesting things about SharePoint is that it allows users to create and set up sites. You can as well add more users and give specified permissions to some (or all). This chapter makes a better explanation and detailed information on managing a site.

How to create a site

Every site is based on templates. The content and basic layout of your site are determined by the template you choose; there are four categories of templates that you can choose from and they are Duet Enterprise, Collaboration, Custom, and Enterprise. Each of this template category contains in itself different kinds of designs which are made for different purposes like Blog, Team Site, Community Site, and Project Site. If you want to create a new site use the following guide:

Step 1. Move to the parent site where you will like your site to be located

Step 2. Click the Settings button

Step 3. Once it opens, select Site settings

Step 4. Click on Sites and workspaces

Step 5. Subsequently, the Sites and Workspaces screen opens. Select Create

Step 6. This opens the New SharePoint Site window. Right in the Title box enter a title for the site

Step 7. Also, in the Description box, enter a description of the site

Step 8. In the URL name box, enter any name you would like to be in the last part of the URL name for the site, keep in mind that you are not meant to put spaces in the Web site address

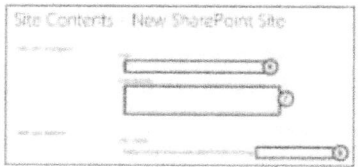

Step 9. With the diverse options available on the category tab, select the desired template which you intend using to create your site. Once that is done, you should add some

libraries, additional lists, pages, and apps based on your preferences.

Step 10. Specify whether or not you want to display your new site on the Top Link Bar and Quick Launch of the parent site. Do this through the Navigation/Navigation Inheritance section.

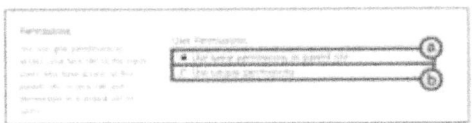

Step 11. Click Create

Setting up groups for the site

You can only use Setup Groups for your Site screen when opting to create unique permissions not inheriting permissions from the parent site. If you had selected use same permissions as parent site (under user permissions) you will skip over this screen. If otherwise, the following steps explains how to set up your unique permission groups.

Choose your permissions for any of these three groups:

i. Visitors: This group can only read the contents on the website but with no permission to contribute or edit the site content.

ii. Members: This set can add contents to the web site and edit only their own contributions.

iii. Owners: This group is in absolute control over the Web site.

The group you choose determines the permissions you give.

How to set up permissions for Visitors

Step 1. Allow people to view the site through the Visitors to this Site section by using an existing group or creating a new group.

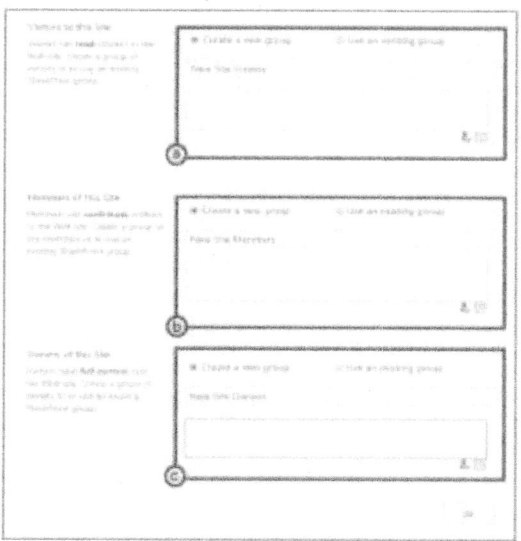

Step 2. After that, a Select People and Groups window will open, enter a group or person's name in the Find field and click Search to search the global directory.

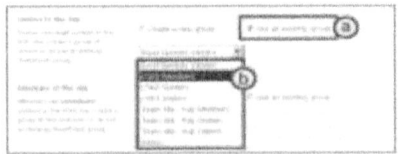

Step 3. Select the name you want to add from the result list that pops up and Click Add. You can as well search and add as many names then click OK once completed.

How to set up permissions for Members

In the section outlined for Members of this Site, use the same steps as mentioned above to give users permissions to contribute to the site. Users in the Members category can view, edit, add, and delete site content.

How to set up permissions for Owners

Similarly, the same step as for the Visitors and Members groups is applicable to the Owners of this Site section. Do this to give users total control of the site.

Once that is done, Click OK.

How to modify site permissions

Whenever you are assigning permission to groups, always consider the security controls you intend to put in position for your site. Permissions are one of the many things that allow you to customize the kind of contents that can be added, viewed, updated, and deleted on your web site (and by who). To determine permissions, you need to first understand the type of actions users will perform on your site. The list below is a compilation of permission levels that you can give to individuals and groups.

> Full Control: This includes full control and all permissions.
> Design: Here, the permissions given are to view, add, approve, update, customize, and delete.
> Edit: This permission level allows users to add, edit, and also delete lists. Also, users can view, add, delete, and update documents and list items.
> Contribute: Viewing, adding, deleting, and updating documents and list items is the only permission granted to users in this category.
> Read: Here, users can view list items and pages and also download documents.
> View Only: This last permission allows users to view list items, pages, and documents. Documents with certain server-side file handlers can only be viewed in the browser but cannot be downloaded.

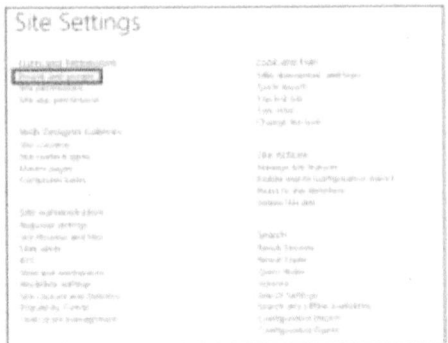

To view site permissions, use the People and Groups link present in the Site Settings window. To make further modifications on your Site, use the following instructions:

How to add a Group or User to a Site

Step 1. Go to the Site and Select the Settings button

Step 2. If you want to access the Site Settings window, click Site Settings

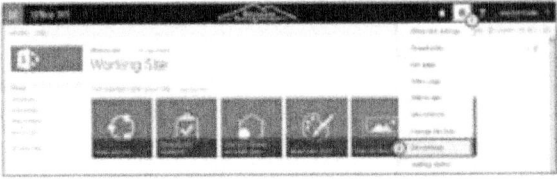

Step 3. In the Site Settings window, Select Site Permissions; subsequently, this opens the Site Permissions window.

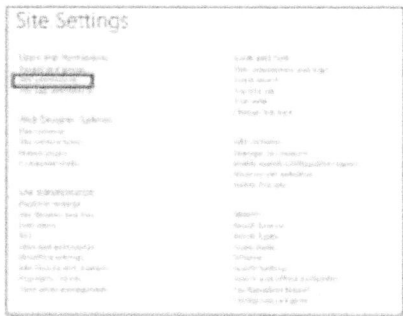

Step 4. Click Grant Permissions in the Ribbon on the Permissions tab.

Step 5. This opens the Share site window. Add your desired members and create an email invitation message to help notify users about their access to the site.

Step 6. Input the name (or names) of the groups/users that you intend adding to the site in the Users/Groups box. SharePoint will search for the names you type using Active Directory.

Step 7. Add an optional personal message alongside the invitation

Step 8. If you want to add users without sending any email invitation or change the default permission level, Select SHOW OPTIONS.

Step 9. Also, if you want to disable the email invitation, click on the checkbox to uncheck Send an email invitation.

Step 11. Click Share after completing the steps.

Step 12. You can as well share with others by clicking the Share button in the toolbar.

How to modify Permissions on a Site

Step 1. Move to the Site and Click SHARE in the toolbar. This opens the share site to allow you to see having access to view your site as well as invite others to your site

Step 2. To send an email to all those having access to your site, click Shared with.

Step 3. Click Email Everyone to create and subsequently send an email to everyone you have shared site permissions with.

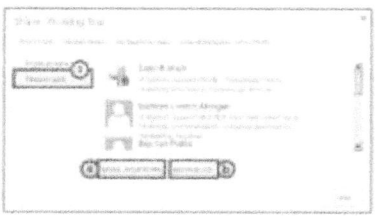

Step 4. To access and change site permissions, click Advanced. This opens the Site Permissions window where you can create a new group, grant permissions to individuals,

33

and edit membership and permission levels to the entire group.

Step 5. To change a group or user, click the checkbox next to the user/group; then click on the Edit User Permissions button on the Ribbon.

Step 6. Confirm the appropriate boxes in the Edit Permissions window; then click OK.

How to check a Group's full permissions

Step 1. Go to the site then click the Settings button.

Step 2. Once the Settings open, Click Site Settings

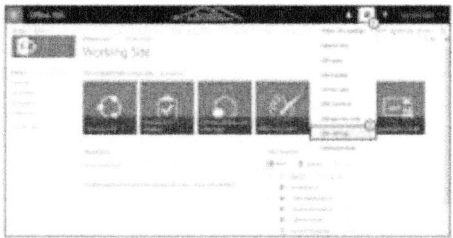

Step 3. Afterward, click People and Groups under the Users and Permissions tab on the Site settings

Step 4. Click the name of the group you wish to view in the Group list.

Step 5. Then, click the drop-down arrow for the group setting and click View Group Permission. This displays a page showing the permission level of the group as well as the URL of each site which the groups have access to.

How to Delete a User from a Group

Step 1. Go to the appropriate site and click on the Settings button.

Step 2. Once the Settings will, Click Site Settings.

Step 3. Under Users and Permissions (on the Site Settings page), Click People and Groups.

Step 4. Continue by clicking on the name of the group you wish to edit in the Group list.

Step 5. Next to the name of the person you want to delete, click the checkbox next to the name; then click the drop-down arrow for more Actions.

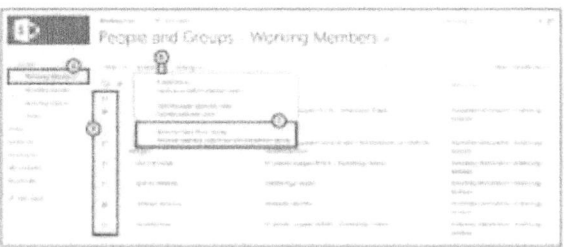

Step 6. Once the Actions pop up, click Remove Users from Group then click OK to complete the action.

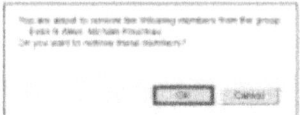

CHAPTER FIVE

Working with pages on SharePoint

One great way to share ideas and information using diverse types of content is through pages. With pages, you can insert images, text, documents, videos, and many more on the same page simultaneously. Site pages are in two separate dimensions (a Web Parts page and a standard page). Web parts page consists of Web Parts in Web Parts zones while a standard page on the other hand contains images, texts, Web parts, and some other elements without formatting tools or zones. Web parts pages usually have predefined layout options which makes use of Web Part zones to aid users' creation of pages.

Note that every SharePoint site has at least one page (the Home Page) which is a Web Parts page. As much as you desire, you can add more pages to a site.

How to create a Web Parts Site Page

Step 1. Click Site Pages in Quick Launch, click Site Pages.

Step 2. Once the Site Pages window appears, click New.
Step 3. Click Web Part Page (the drop-down window that appears shows the kind of pages you can create, so you can choose some other pages based on your preferences)

Editing a Web Part Site Page

All pages are made up of series of building blocks known as Web Parts. The default page set for a Team site has in it one Web part through which you can add and remove contents to the page. However, there are many ways and options through which you can modify and organize the layout to make your page look just as you want it. You can include the countless type of contents like videos, pictures, app parts, links, and many other Web parts to your page.

Once you have successfully created your page, SharePoint takes you to the page Edit window. This is where you can organize tabs and position media in the best order. Here, you will see the Ribbon which is set into diverse groupings and tabs with the use of drop-down boxes and buttons which you can utilize to edit your page. By default settings, you are initially launched to the Format Text tab where you can start building your page by formatting and entering text, selecting layouts for your page, choosing desired styles for your text and elements, and many more.

Saving a page

After adding content to your page, what comes next is saving your page. To this effect, there are diverse options for saving your page with the use of Format Text or Page tabs.

Step 1. Click the Page tab in the Ribbon

Step 2. Click on Save drop-dow. This shows the following options

a. Save: This helps you save all changes made on the page and exit the edit mode as well.

b. Save and Keep Editing: This saves all changes made on the page and lets you keep editing

c. Stop Editing: This option exits the editing mode on the page. You will be asked whether you want to discard or save changes.

Ways to check out a Page

If you want to keep your page confidential and keep other users from editing your page while you are working on in edit mode, always check out the page. When you check out a page, it becomes impossible for anyone to edit it while it is checked out. To do this, start by:

Step 1. click Check out in the ribbon. Subsequently, this action changes the status of your page to Editable and Checked out; that way the page can only be edited by the user who checked it out (which is you at that moment).

Step 2. All changes made on the page will only become visible to other users when the page is changed from checked out to check-in using the Check-in button.

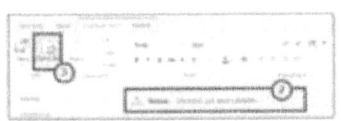

Changing the Layout

If you want to give your page a different look, change the layout. To change your page's layout to a better one, use the lines below.

Step 1. On the Ribbon, click the Text Layout button in the Format Text tab. This action displays the drop-down box which shows many layout options available at the moment.

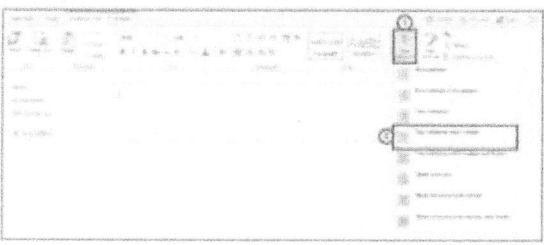

Step 2. Choose any of the layouts you will like on your page. Instantly, the Web part sections get the update upon your selection.

How to add a Web Part to a Page Zone

Step 1. On the Ribbon, click on the Insert tab

Step 2. Click Web Part

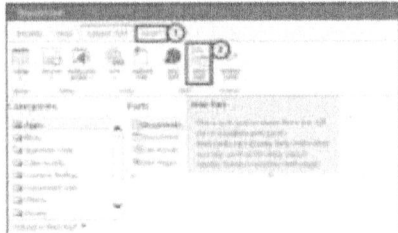

Step 3. Select the zone where you want the Web Part to be inserted

Step 4. Choose one category from th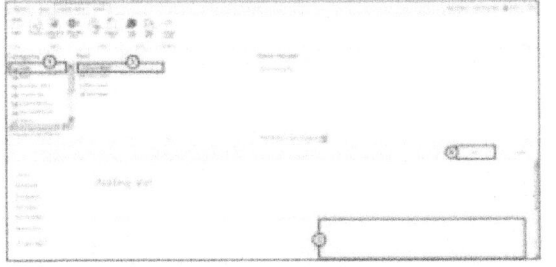e
Categories list

Step 5. Select a Web Part from the displayed Web Parts list

Step 6. Click Add, this shows the Web part in your selected zone.

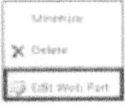

Step 7. Click OK once you are done making changes.

Deleting a Web Part

If you want to delete a Web Part, use the steps below:

Step 1. Move the mouse pointer to the top right-hand corner of the Web part you intend deleting.

Step 2. Then, Click on the drop-down arrow which appears.

Step 3. Click Delete to get rid of it.

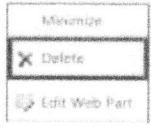

Adding Individual Content Items

Whenever you add a web part to your page, it is noteworthy that you are including a specific kind of content by the nature of the Web Part or item that you select in the Ribbon.

Step 1. Click the area inside the Page Content

Step 2. Select the zone you want to use

Step 3. On the Ribbon, click on the Insert tab

Step 4. Select the button on the Ribbon for the particular item that you intend inserting.

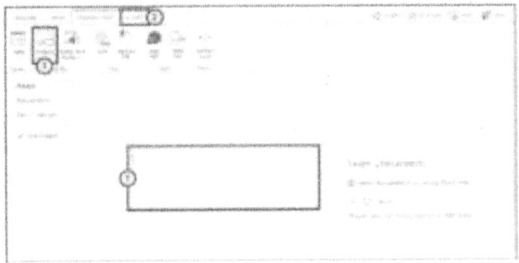

Step 5. Select the file location of the picture you wish to insert with the use of the drop-down menu

Step 6. Click Browse to help you locate your file.

Step 7. Click on the File you would want to insert and select Open.

Step 8. Once the file pops up in the Upload Image window, click OK. This uploads the image to your site page.

Now that the image is on your site page, you can edit and position it whichever way you want. You can as well add more texts and elements to the page.

Editing a Page After Initial Configuration

Step 1. Go to the page which you wish to edit.

Step 2. Click on the Page tab

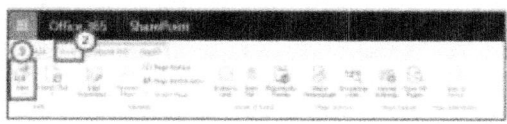

Step 3. Then, click the Edit button

Step 4. Select the zone you want to edit.

Step 5. On the Ribbon, Use the various tools on the Format Text tab to edit and configure the text in every zones of your page.

Step 6. If you want to insert media, links, tables, apps, files, and Web parts; do this by using the tools on the Insert tab. You can also embed codes in various zones of your page.

Step 7. Once finished, click the Save by clicking the Page tab.

CHAPTER SIX

Working with documents on SharePoint library

In SharePoint, all documents are stored in a number of containers called Document Libraries instead of folders. However, this document libraries van also be divided into subdivisions like the Document Library itself or even folders. To locate the document library, you can look up to it among the listings in the Quick Launch somewhere on the left-hand side of your site window. If you want to view the documents in a document library, just click on it to display the list of documents stored in that particular library; vital information about the document like the name, the date of creation, the author and many more (this information is referred to as metadata).

Creating a New Document in a SharePoint Document Library

It is noteworthy that SharePoint has integration with PowerPoint, Excel, Microsoft Word, and OneNote. In that regard, SharePoint makes use of all these online applications in the creation of new documents which will then open in the version of the Office Online which is very suitable to the file (for instance all Microsoft word documents will open in word online). After creating the file in the online app, you can proceed and open the file with any corresponding Office program you have installed on your computer.

If you want to create a new document:

Step 1. Select the name of the Document Library where you want to save a new document through the Quick Launch

Step 2. Click New

Step 3. Click the Office program you want to create from the list that appears

Step 4. Instantly, Word Online opens a blank document for you to create with

Step 5. If you want to change the document name, simply click document name from inside Word Online and proceed by entering a new document name

Step 6. Once finished, click on the site name before Word Online; this way, your new document pops up in the chosen SharePoint library

How to upload documents to a SharePoint Document Library

The most simple and fastest way to upload files to your SharePoint library is simply by dragging the desired file into your document library file list. Automatically, this file is uploaded to your chosen library. Interestingly, there are many other ways to upload documents into your SharePoint document library as stated below:

Step 1. Click on the Document library you wish to have the document stored via the Quick Launch panel.

Step 2. Click on all the files you would be uploading and drag them to any location on the library page (where you want to have them).

Step 3. The file is uploaded to where you have selected

You can also upload files and/or folders by following the steps below:

Step 1. Through the Quick Launch, click on the document library where you would like to have your document stored

Step 2. Click Upload

Step 3. Once the File Explorer will appears, select all the files from your computer then click Open.

Step 4. The selected files are thereby uploaded (you can check the toolbar to monitor the progress of the selected files).

How to open documents in a SharePoint Document Library

One feature on SharePoint that allows you to access diverse Microsoft Office files and also edit them as you wish is the SharePoint Document Libraries. With this feature, you can edit your files Online with the Microsoft Office Online series of tools or you can decide to open them by using the desktop version of any Microsoft Office package. In the following lines, you will see how to open a word document online as well as how to keep editing with the desktop version of Word.

Step 1. Open the document by clicking the document name via the Document Library list. This will automatically open the document in the Office Online version.

Step 2. Click Edit

Note: You have two options displayed on your screen when you click Edit

a. Edit in Browser: This launch the file to an Office Online where you can proceed with the document and edit with your browser.

b. Edit in Word: If you have installed the Microsoft Office to your computer, the file will be reverted to a corresponding program for opening and subsequent editing.

Step 3. Click on the SharePoint site name beside Word Online once you are done editing; this will launch you back to your document library

How to Check Out Documents

A document library that has been configured requires you to check it in and out before any editing can be made on a SharePoint document. When you check out a document, you prevent any other person from having access to open or edit that same file until you check the document in again i.e., when you are done editing. Immediately you check the document in again, it becomes available to opened, edited, and even checked in and out by someone else. To enjoy this feature and prevent anyone else from opening the document you are working on, check it out with the guides below.

To check out a document:

Step 1. Start by placing a checkmark right in front of the document you intend checking out

Step 2. Then, click the Eclipse on the Toolbar. This reveals some options through the drop-down menu.

Step 3. Click Check out in the drop-down menu that pops. This shows a green and white arrow on an icon next to the selected document

How to Check-In Documents

To check a document back in after editing it, use the steps below

Step 1. First place a checkmark right in front of the document you intend checking in

Step 2. Then, click the Eclipse on the Toolbar. This reveals some options through the drop-down menu.

Step 3. Click Check-In, in the drop-down menu that pops. This shows a green and white arrow on an icon next to the selected document

How to Move Files into Folders

Step 1. First, create a new folder by clicking New in the toolbar

Step 2. Click folder in the drop-down option that displays

Step 3. Enter the name of the folder you want to create

Step 4. Click Create

Step 5. Drag a file into the folder to move it therein (you can also move multiple files by clicking the space to the left side of the file and then drag the group into the folder

How to Move Files from One Folder to Another

Step 1. Select all the files you want to move

Step 2. Click on Move to in the toolbar on your screen

Step 3. Click a folder destination in the file location options that appear on your right

Step 4. Click Move here to move all files to the newly selected location

How to Copy Files from One Folder to Another

Step 1. Select all the files you want to move

Step 2. Click on Copy via the toolbar

Step 3. Click the folder destination you want to copy to from the File location options that appears on your right

Step 4. Complete action by clicking Copy here

How to use File Explorer to Move or Copy Between Libraries

File explorer view allows users to drop and drag files into libraries, copy and move files, create folders, and also delete any files in your library. However, this feature is only accessible through Internet Explorer. To utilize the View in File Explorer use the guide below.

Step 1. Go to the document library which contains the files you want to move or copy

Step 2. Click on the Documents drop-down

Step 3. Select the View in File Explorer; this opens a Microsoft File Explorer window for access to the original library

Step 4. Move to the document library where you wish to move and copy the files/folders

Step 5. Repeat steps 2 and 3; this opens two Explorer windows

Step 6. Highlight the Folder and Files you want to move or copy

Step 7 Copy the files by right-clicking them and selecting copy; then go back to the destination library window to right-click and select Paste.

Step 8. Move the files you want by dragging them into the destination library window.

CHAPTER SEVEN

All SharePoint list functionality

Via an end-user perspective, discussions will be made in this chapter about Lists and some other value-added features aside from lists like Validation, Views, and many more. When an end-user creates content with the use of SharePoint, such information is stored in the form of lists.

De facto, lists are the real data storage mechanism within SharePoint, providing a well accessible user interface in terms of adding, listing, editing and deleting items or better still view individual items.

The following lines shows how to add a contact list

Step 1. Open your SharePoint site and Navigate to the Site Contents page. Here you have access to view the present lists, contents, and libraries and also add new contents by clicking add app.

Note: The things you can add to your site includes:

A custom list which can be used to define the schema
Creating a new document library

Adding pictures, forms, wiki pages, announcement list, links list, calendar, contact list and more

Step 2. Select Contacts list

Step 3. Click the Create button on your screen (now you have your site contact lists created).

Step 4. Click New Item link to add more content to this list

Step 5. Click Stop editing once you are done editing; this takes you out of badge edit mode

The most interesting thing about SharePoint is that it provides a lot of functionality for lists. SharePoint also provides much storage for list data making it able to customize the list schema as well as the ability to add, view, edit, and delete list items. Also, there are many other functionality available on SharePoint like content approval, simple validation at both the field and list level, creating views on list data, item versioning, and many more.

Views

Due to the increment in the number of items from 4 to 50 and then to 100; perhaps 500. Glancing at the list and getting instant information is more difficult than ever. In response to this, SharePoint allows users to create many Views on lists; this allows you to filter out the less important information. This way users can:

Sort the field values.
Group information.

Get totals.

Also, there are many different ways to present information. In the aspect of lists, when users create a list, one View is given by default. This is called the All Items View.

Lookup Fields

With Lookup Fields and list relations, users can create a new list for holding diverse information about courses as stated below:

Step 1 – Navigate to Site Contents

Step 2: Select dd an app

Step 3. Click the Custom List.

Step 4 – Specify the list Courses you want then click Create

Step 5. Open the Courses list (there is one column called Title, which will represent the title of the course)

Step 6 – Create a second column, this will hold the name of the author.

Step 7. On the Ribbon, Go to LIST on the Ribbon.

Step 8. Click Create Column.

Step 9. Name the column

Step 10. Specify which field from which list that would be showing to the user.

Step 11. The course is created

List Data Storage

The data meant for lists is usually stored in columns and rows. All content database has one table, this table is meant for storing data for lists; you can as well relate the lists together and make from validating by enforcing relational integrity.

A lot of people usually assume that lots of abilities of a relational database lies with lists and some other set of lists which makes it becomes something similar to a relational database but in reality it is not.

The list is more like those set of Excel worksheets that allows you to have the worksheets linked with the other. Here you can enforce some validations on cells and columns with the aid of some simple form. In essence, sets of the list in SharePoint is more like Excel spreadsheets and not as a relational database.

CHAPTER EIGHT

Other SharePoint features and elements

In this chapter, we will take a look at features and elements. Features are in some ways the component model in SharePoint. They allow you to define logical units of functionality.

For example, you might want to have the ability within a site –

> To create a list with a specific schema,
> Have a page that will show the data from that list, and then
> Have a link or a menu option somewhere within the site to navigate to that page.

You could create a feature, which defines the logical grouping of functionality. The individual pieces of functionality are defined by elements.

So there would be an element which –

> Creates the list and sets the schema.
> Provisions the page into your SharePoint site, and
> Creates the menu option or the link.

The feature defines the unit and then the elements define the individual pieces of functionality inside of that unit. We discussed the three kinds of elements –

> A list instance to create a list.
> A module to provide a page.
> Custom action to create a menu option or a link.

However, there are many other kinds of elements that can be created within SharePoint. Another important concept to understand about features is that of activation and deactivation.

For example, if an end-user wants the above-mentioned functionality to be added to his site, he would activate the corresponding feature that would create the list, add the menu option or link, and provision the page into their site. Later he could deactivate the feature to remove the functionality.

It is important to note that on deactivation of a feature, some elements are automatically removed. For example, SharePoint would automatically remove the menu option or link, which is defined by a custom action.

Others are not removed automatically. Therefore, in our case, the list instance and the page would not be removed automatically.

Hence, as a developer, you need to understand what elements get removed automatically and which ones do not.

If you want to remove the ones that do not get removed automatically, you can write in code in a feature receiver.

Let us look at working with features and elements. We will start with the end-users view of features.

Step 1 − Open your SharePoint site.

Step 2 − To go to the Site Settings, you have two links that enable you to manage features.

> The first link Manage Site features are under Site Actions, which enables you to manage site scope features.
> The other link Site collection features under Site Collection Administration, which enables you to manage site collection scope features.

Step 3 − If you click on either of these links, you will be taken to a page, which shows the currently active and inactive features. For each of the features, you have an option to activate or deactivate the feature.

Let us look at a simple example by creating a new SharePoint Solutions Empty Project.

Step 1 − Let us call this FeaturesAndElements and click OK.

Step 2 − Specify the site you want to use and select the Deploy as a farm solution option and then click Finish.

The first thing we want to create is a feature. In the Solution Explorer, you can see a Features folder, which is currently empty.

Step 3 − Right-click on the Features folder and choose Add Feature. It creates a Feature named Feature1, and it opens up the Feature designer. The default Title is the title of the project, plus the title of the feature.

Step 4 − Rename the feature from Feature1 to Sample.

> Title and Description are what the user sees on the page where they activate and deactivate the features. Set the Title to Sample Feature and the Description to Adds the Contacts list and the page is used to view the list. The other thing we need to set is the Scope of the feature, which is the activation scope.
> It can be Farm, a WebApplication, a Site collection, or a Site. In this case, we are going to provision a list and a page. Since, both live in a SharePoint site, so we will pick Web here.

Step 5 − Let us start adding features in our elements. The first element will be the list and we will create a contacts list. Right-click on your project and choose Add → New Item...

Step 6 − Select List in the middle pane and enter Contacts in the name field. Click Add.

Step 7 − You will see the List Creation Wizard. Create a list called Contacts based on the Contacts list. Click Finish to create the list or at least create the element, which will eventually create the list.

Step 8 − This designer is just an XML editor. Open the file Elements.xml under Contacts and add the data.

Step 9 − Now we want to have a page, which shows data from this list. Right-click on your project and choose Add → New Item... Choose Module in the middle pane, enter SitePage in the name field, and click Add.

Step 10 − Rename the text file to Contacts.aspx and replace the code

Step 11 − Go to your project and right-click, and choose Add → New Item...

Step 12 − Come back to Elements.xml under Action and replace the code −

Step 13 − Double click on the Feature, you will see the Feature designer. Feature designer is a fancy editor of the Feature Manifest, which is an XML document.

Step 14 − Go to the Project Properties by going to the SharePoint tab. Change the Deployment Configuration to No Activation.

Step 15 − Right-click on your project in Solution Explorer and choose Deploy. It will package up all the stuff in your project and deploy it out to your SharePoint Development Farm.

Step 16 − Go to the SharePoint site and Refresh it. Go to the Site Settings → Site Actions.

Step 17 − Select the Manage site features because your Custom Feature was Web scoped and you will see your Sample Feature.

Step 18 − Click Contact and the data that we had on the list will be displayed.

Step 19 − Go to the Site actions menu. There is an option to navigate to the Contacts page. That is our CustomAction.

Step 20 − If you click Contacts, then you will see your site page, showing the data from the Contacts list.

CHAPTER NINE

The SharePoint Azure Platform

In this chapter, we will be covering the Microsoft Azure Platform. Microsoft Azure is Microsoft's cloud platform technology, which is in itself a very powerful technology. It is not just a place to deploy your code, but it is a whole set of services exists that you as a developer can use in your SharePoint solution development.

Cloud Computing

To understand Microsoft Azure, you must first know a bit about the cloud. Cloud computing is all about leveraging the Web as a set of resources for the development and deployment of your solutions. Traditionally, cloud computing has been defined as a category of services. They are –

> Infrastructure as a Service (IAAS)
> Platform as a Service (PAAS)
> Software as a Service (SAAS)

Each one of these categories is different in the context of development. For instance, you might think –

> IAAS as hosted virtual machines (VMs) you manage remotely.

> PAAS as where you deploy code, data, binary large objects (BLOBs), web apps, and other application artifacts to a cloud-based environment (such as Windows Server 2012 R2 and IIS).
> SAAS as subscription-based services that you can sign up to use, for example, Office 365.

Although these three categories of services dominate the way in which the cloud is characterized, the cloud has four generally accepted pillars –

> Pool resources with other cloud users.
> Manage your own services and apps through the management portal.
> Apps and services can grow and contract with your business name
> Pay for only what you use in regards to the cloud.

Azure Platform Overview

The Microsoft Azure platform is composed of many different services. You can leverage them in your application design, deployment, and management such as Data, Service, and Integration, which is the Client layer in any application that consumes the services within Microsoft Azure.

Data Layer

In the Data layer, there are a number of different types of data storage mechanisms or features that map directly to data storage which contains both non-relational and relational.

Non-relational Feature

The non-relational storage features enable you —

> To store assets such as virtual machine images or images or videos in Blobs
> Create non-relational tables
> Manage message queues along a service bus, and manage data caching in your distributed applications

Relational Feature

The relational data features are as follows —

> The core Azure SQL Database, which is the cloud version for the on-premises SQL Server
> Reporting services (SQL Reporting)
> The ability to stream near real-time data streams from data transactions (Stream Insight)

Services Layer

The Services layer contains a number of default services that you can use when building your solutions, ranging from Media Services to core Cloud Services such as —

> Creating websites
> Worker role classes
> Leveraging Hadoop on Microsoft Azure to process Big Data requests

For many of these services, you can use baked-in functionality and a set of APIs within your application. For example, if you want to build a multimedia learning solution, you could leverage the Media Services —

> To upload WMVs
> Transcode them to MP4s
> Save them to BLOB storage
> Create a public URL for access and then stream them from Microsoft Azure

Integration Layer

The Integration layer contains some fundamental services such as —

> Geo-replicated content delivery network (CDN)
> Traffic Manager
> Virtual Private Network, which enables you to connect a virtual machine to your on-premises system
> Workflow and business process and integration services

All of these capabilities enable you to integrate systems or secure them.

Azure Apps

Microsoft Azure is not just about services. Azure is an ever-evolving cloud platform that has a set of tools and SDKs that enable you to get started with the development of cloud applications quickly.

To start with Microsoft Azure you need the following —

Visual Studio latest
Microsoft Azure subscription
Microsoft Azure subscription

Step 1 − Let us have a look at a simple example in which we will deploy our web application to Microsoft Azure by creating a new ASP.NET MVC application.

Step 2 − Click Ok and you will see the dialog box. Select MVC template, check Host in the Cloud checkbox and then click OK.

Step 3 − When the Configure Microsoft Azure Web App Settings dialog appears, make sure that you are signed in to Azure. If you are not signed in, then first sign in.

Step 4 − Enter the desired information as shown below. Select Create a new server from the Database server dropdown list.

Step 5 − You will see the additional field. Enter the Database server, username, and password and click Ok.

Once the project is created, run your application and you will see that it is running on the localhost.

Step 6 − To deploy these applications to Azure, right-click on the project in solution explorer, and select Publish.

Step 7 − You will see the dialog box. Click the Microsoft Azure Web Apps.

Step 8 − Select your application name from the Existing Web Apps and click OK.

Step 9 − Click the Validate Connection button to check for the connection on Azure.

Step 10 − Click Next to continue.

Now you will see that the connection string is generated for you already, by default.

Step 11 − Click Next to continue.

Step 12 − To check all the files and DLLs, which we will be publishing to Azure, click Start Preview.

Step 13 − Click Publish to publish your application.

Once the application is successfully published to Azure, you will see the message in the output window.

You will also see that your application is now running from the cloud.

SharePoint Apps and Microsoft Azure

SharePoint and Microsoft Azure are two sizeable platforms unto themselves. SharePoint is one of Microsoft's leading server productivity platforms or the collaborative platform for the enterprise and the Web.

Microsoft Azure is Microsoft's operating system in the cloud. Separately, they have their own strengths, market viability, and developer following.

Together, they provide many powerful benefits. They are −

> They help expand how and where you deploy your code and data.
> They increase opportunities to take advantage of the Microsoft Azure while at the same time reducing the storage and failover costs of on-premises applications.
> They provide you with new business models and offerings that you can take to your customers to increase your own solution offerings.

In SharePoint 2010, Azure and SharePoint were two distinct platforms and technologies, which could be integrated easily enough, but they were not part of the same system. However, in SharePoint 2013 this has changed.

SharePoint 2013 introduces different types of cloud applications. In fact, you can build two types of Azure integrated applications.

The first type of application is Autohosted, and the second is Provider-hosted (sometimes referred to as self-hosted).

The major difference between the two is −

> Autohosted applications natively support a set of Azure features such as Web Sites and SQL Database with the SharePoint development and deployment experience.
> Provider-hosted applications are meant to integrate with a broader set of web technologies and standards

than Autohosted applications, one of which is Microsoft Azure.

Thus, you can take advantage of the entire Microsoft Azure stack when building Provider hosted apps that use Azure.

CHAPTER TEN

Other SharePoint Apps

In this chapter, we will be covering SharePoint Apps. The app model is a new development deployment and hosting model for extensions to SharePoint. As a developer in SharePoint, we have the option of using the solutions model, either farm or sandbox solutions, or using the app model.

Microsoft documentation and guidance suggest that you favor the app model over the solutions model and that might be very valid guidance. However, you have to consider that the app model, which is a significant addition to SharePoint 2013, while the solutions model has been around since SharePoint 2007.

Therefore, the knowledge base for development with the solutions model is significantly better than the current state of the knowledge base for developing apps.

Apps have not been around long enough for people to share their real-world experiences using it. I think it is very important that you learn the app model and its strengths and weaknesses.

App Characteristics

App characteristics are given below −

The first and probably the most important, from the developer viewpoint, is that all the codes in an app are executed outside of the SharePoint server. This means that the code is either JavaScript running in the users' browser or it is the code that is running on some external server.

Since all the code is running outside of SharePoint, communication with SharePoint is done via web services, which means you are using the Client Object Model or the REST API.

There are no circumstances where you can use the Server Object Model in a SharePoint app.

Once you are finished building your app, you are either going to put it in the public app store or local app catalog. This requires a review process and there are some rules, which you need to follow to make your app eligible to go to the public app store.

The other option is to put your app in a local app catalog, which is just a site collection, within your web application, that has been configured by central administration to be the app catalog.

Once your app has been deployed to the store of the catalog, users with site collection owner permission can install it in SharePoint sites.

App Types

There are different types of apps that you can build, which are as follows −

SharePoint-Hosted App

The first is the SharePoint-Hosted App. As the name suggests, this kind of app is hosted on your SharePoint farm.

Important features are −

> It is hosted in a child site of the site where it is installed and this child site behaves for the most part, like other sites.
> It can contain lists, libraries, pages, content types, and so on.

The basics of building a SharePoint-Hosted App are similar to the basics of building a SharePoint Solution.

> We can add elements to that feature and those elements are defined using CAML.
> For many of the elements, we have designers in Visual Studio.
> We can add site pages.
> We can add server controls to those site pages.
> We cannot add code behind those site pages, but we can add JavaScript code.

Now once you get beyond the basics, things start to get less and less similar.

Cloud-Hosted Apps

The other two types of apps, Provider-Hosted and Auto-Hosted, are categorized together as Cloud-Hosted Apps.

Important features are —

> These apps live in a site external to SharePoint.
> The big difference between Provider-Hosted and Auto-Hosted is who is going to create and manage this external site —
> In a Provider-Hosted App, that is you or your organization.
> In an Auto-Hosted App, that is Microsoft.
> Building a Cloud-Hosted App is the same as building any other website.

If you are a .NET developer, you are probably using MVC or WebForms. However, you are not limited to those technologies. You can build a Cloud-Hosted App with whatever web technology you want. When you are finished building your app, in the Provider-Hosted scenario, you will deploy the app up to your site the way you would do for any other website.

In the Auto-Hosted scenario, you use Visual Studio to create an app package. It is an app equivalent to a solution package and then you can upload that to SharePoint Online and a site. If necessary, a database will be provisioned for you to host your app.

Auto-Hosted Apps can only be used with SharePoint Online, they are not supported with an on-premises farm.

You can see an example of a SharePoint hosted application when you open Visual Studio as sighted below.

Step 1 – Open Visual Studio

Step 2- Select the File then, New

Step 3- Click the Project menu.

Step 4 – In the left pane select Templates then Click Visual C#

Step 5- Select Office/SharePoint and then click App for SharePoint in the middle pane.

Step 6- Enter the Name in the Name field then, Click OK. You will see a dialog box.

Step 7 – Go to the SharePoint admin center and copy the SharePoint URL.

Step 8 – Paste the URL in the New App for SharePoint dialog box

Step 9 – Then, click Next, and this will open the Connect to SharePoint dialog box where you will need to log in.

Step 10 – Enter your credentials then click the Sign in button. After you are successfully logged in to the SharePoint site, you will see a dialog box

Step 11 − Click Finish. Click the AppMenifest.xml file in the Solution Explorer, Once the project is created.

Step 12 − Click the Permissions tab. A Scope dropdown list will pop up.

Step 13 − In the Scope dropdown list, select Web, which is the scope of permissions that you are configuring. In the Permission drop-down list, select Read, which is the type of permission you are configuring.

Step 14 − Then, go to the Solution Explorer, right-click the project and select Publish. Click the Package the app button. This builds your SharePoint-hosted app and prepares it for you for deployment to your SharePoint site.

Step 15 − Move to your SharePoint online site.

Step 16 − In the left pane, click Apps for SharePoint. This will open a new page.

Step 17 − Drag your files here to upload.

Step 18- Once the file is uploaded, you will see a new page

Step 19 − Click Site Contents in the left pane then Click on add an app icon

Step 20 − From Your Organization in the left pane, select your Apps and you will see that the app is available to be installed. Click the app.

Step 21 – A dialog box opens when you click the App; Click Trust it.

Step 22 – This shows you that the app is installed. Once the installation is complete, you can now click the app.

You can see an example of an Autohosted application when you click to create a new project as sighted below.

Step 1 – Select App for SharePoint then click OK.

Step 2 – Select Autohosted.

Step 3 – Select ASP.NET MVC Web Application and click Finish.

Once the project is created, publish your app. The rest of the steps are the same as given for the SharePoint-hosted option.

CHAPTER ELEVEN

Sandbox Solutions

In this chapter, we will be covering the deployment of Sandbox Solutions. Deployment of a Sandbox Solution is quite simpler than the deployment of a Farm solution.

It is similar to uploading a document to a document library. When you finish your development, you are going to take the solution package and instead of giving it to your SharePoint administrator, you will give it to an end-user, someone with site-collection owner privilege. Then they will take the package and upload it to the site-collection solution gallery.

Just like with Farm solutions, the tools in Visual Studio automate this deployment process, during development.

A guide on how to create a Sandbox Solution Deployment is given below. The process is somewhat simpler than Farm solution deployment.

Step 1 − Change Contacts list name back to just Contacts in FeaturesAndElements project.

Step 2 − Retract the solution by right-clicking on the project and choosing Retract.

Step 3 – Go back to the Visual Studio project, click the project in the Solution Explorer, and then go to the properties window.

Step 4 - Change Sandbox Solution from False to True.

Note: This gives us an indication that some of the items you added to the Visual Studio project will not work with Sandbox solutions and some of the SharePoint APIs. Some of the types within the SharePoint Server Object Model are not compatible with Sandbox solutions.

Click Yes to make the change. In this case, building a sandbox solution is the same as building a farm solution, but the deployment process is completely different.

With the sandbox solution, instead of deploying files up into the SharePoint system folders, we deploy into the SharePoint content database.

Step 5 – Go to the Site settings. And find the Solutions gallery Under the Web Designer Galleries.

Step 6 – Click the Solutions link and you will see a page where we deploy our sandbox solutions.

Step 7 – Go back to Visual Studio, right-click and select Publish to File System.

Step 8- Click the Publish button to publish the New Solution Package to the package folder.

Step 9 – Go to the SharePoint site then Click the Upload Solution button option on the Ribbon.

Step 10 – Browse to your FeaturesAndElements solution. Click OK.

Step 11 – Click the Activate button to activate the sandbox solution

Step 12 – Go to the Manage site features.

This will now show you your Sample Feature and when you click Activate, you will get the same behavior as seen before.

CHAPTER TWELVE

SharePoint Packaging & Deploying

In this chapter, we will be covering the packaging and Deploying of the SharePoint solution. The first step in the deployment of a SharePoint solution is the creation of a Solution Package.

A Solution Package is a CAB file with WSP extension, which contains all the files required to implement the Features in your Visual Studio project.

The files required to implement the Features include –

> The feature manifest.
> Any element manifests.
> The dll, which contains the compiled managed code.
> Associated files like web pages, user controls, and web paired files.

Another file contained in the solution package is the solution manifest. The solution manifest is a catalog of the files contained in the package. For Farm solutions, it also contains deployment instructions.

Just like with the Feature manifest, Visual Studio automatically creates and maintains the solution manifest as you modify your project. You can see the solution manifest using the solution designer.

In addition to creating and maintaining the solution manifest, Visual Studio is also automatically creating the solution package for our project. It does this behind the scenes every time you deploy your work for debugging.

The generated solution package is placed in the same folder as the dll, so that will be the bin debug or the bin release folder. To view the contents of this file in Windows Explorer, just change the extension from WSP to CAB and then double click on the file.

Let us have a look at an example in which we will examine the solution packages associated with the SharePoint solution projects we have created in the previous chapter. Let us start with the features and elements project we have created earlier.

As noted earlier that in the project, we have one Feature, called Sample. This Feature references three-element manifests Contacts, SitePage, and Action.

You can also see that Action has the Element manifest, Contacts has its Element manifest, SitePage has the Element manifest, and a web page, which provisions this web page into the site. Hence, we should expect the solution package to contain the Feature manifest, the three Element Manifests, the web page, and also the assembly that is created when we build the project.

Step 1 − In the solution explorer, right-click on your project.

Step 2- Choose Open Folder in File Explorer.

Step 3 − Go to the bin and open the Debug folder; this will show you the solution package.

Step 4 − Make a copy of it, then change the extension of the Copy file from wsp to the cab.

Step 5 − Double-click the cab file to open it and you will see the files. You will also see the Feature manifest, three Element manifests, the aspx page, the dll, and one other additional file, which is the Solution manifest.

Step 6 − In the Solution Explorer, you will see a folder called Package; expand it, you will see another file called Package.package. Double-click the latter file and you will see the solution designer.

The solution manifest for this proxy is simple. It just indicates that there is an Assembly that needs to be deployed called FeaturesandElemenest.dll and we will be deploying that to the GlobalAssemblyCache.

It also indicates we have one feature with this Feature Manifest. If we navigate back to the Feature and look at its Manifest, it indicates there are the three Element manifest, and our aspx page.

Farm Solution Deployment

Now that we know, what solution packages are and what they contain, we need to learn how to deploy them.

To deploy a Farm solution, you give the solution package created by Visual Studio to your SharePoint administrator. They will use either PowerShell or Central Administration or a combination of both tools to deploy the package.

To deploy a farm solution, use the guide below

Step 1 – Go to Features and elements in the Visual Studio project.

Step 2 – Go to the List Designer then change the Title to Contacts-Change 1 and click the Save button.

Step 3 – Navigate to the project properties then select SharePoint in the left pane. Choose the Default option from the dropdown list in the Active Deployment Configuration option,

Step 4 – In Solution Explorer, right-click the project then choose Deploy. Once the deployment is finished, refresh your site and this will show you the changes made.

CHAPTER THIRTEEN

Feature/Event Receiver

In this chapter, we will learn to add code handle. Code handles are events that are raised when a Feature is activated or deactivated. In other words, we will be examining Feature Receivers.

The Visual Studio project that we created in the last chapter had one Feature and when it was activated, it provisioned our Contacts list, our site page, and the link to the site page.

However, when the Feature is deactivated, SharePoint only removes the link, the site page, and the Contacts list still remain.

We can write the code when the Feature is deactivated to remove the list and the page if we want to. In this chapter, we will learn how to remove content and elements, when a Feature is deactivated.

To handle the events for a Feature, we need a Feature Receiver. To get the Feature receiver:

Step 1 – Right-click on the Feature in the Solution Explorer

Step 2: Choose Add Event Receiver.

The Events of a Feature are used when it is being –

> Activated
> Deactivated
> Installed
> Uninstalled
> Upgrading

Afterward, you need to attach that class as the event handler for the specific item. For instance, if there is an event handler that handles list events, you need to attach that class to the list.

In that case, we will handle two Features –

> When the feature is activated and
> When it is being deactivated.

Step 3 – Then implement the FeatureActivated and FeatureDeactivated methods

Step 4 – Afterwards right-click on the Project then choose to deploy. This will show you a Deployment Conflict warning.

Step 5 – Go back to SharePoint then refresh your site and navigate to Site Actions

Step 6- Go Site settings and click Manage site features

Step 7- Select the Sample feature.

Step 8 – Activate Sample feature and you will see the Announcements list

Note – If you deactivate your Sample Feature then you will notice that the Announcements list goes away.

Step 9 – Reactivate the feature, Go to Announcements, and then Add a new announcement.

CHAPTER FOURTEEN

Server Object Model

In this chapter, we will take a look at the SharePoint Server Object Model. You use the SharePoint Server Object Model when you are writing code that will run inside the context of SharePoint. Some common examples would be the code-behind in a page or a web part, event handlers behind a feature or a list, timer jobs, etc.

Features of Server Object Model

Following are the key features of the Server Object Model:

> You can use the Server Object Model if you are programming an ASP.NET application inside the same application pool that is used by SharePoint.
> Server Object Model can be used if you are developing a client application such as console or Windows forms or a WPF app that will run on a SharePoint server.
> You cannot use the Server Object Model to connect remotely to a SharePoint Server.
> When you want to use the Server Object Model, you refer to Microsoft.SharePoint assembly. There are other assemblies, which make up the Server Object Model, but Microsoft.SharePoint is the main one.

The core types that you will use most commonly map to the components that you use as an end-user, so things like site collections, sites, lists, libraries, and list items are represented by the types SPSite, SPWeb, SPList, SPDocumentLibrary, and SPListItem.

The type and the Server Object Model that represents a site collection is SPSite and the type that represents a SharePoint site in the Server Object Model is SPWeb. Therefore, when you go from the end-user terms to the developer terms, you will just have to do that mental mapping.

Now when you first start using SharePoint, it can be confusing because the site is so overloaded and it means opposite things in the end-user and developer vocabularies, not to mention the web vocabulary.

Let us have a look at a simple example of the Server Object Model.

Step 1 – Open Visual Studio

Step 2- Create a new project from File

Step 3- Select New

Step 4- Click Project menu option

Step 5 – Select Windows from Templates

Step 6- Click Visual C# in the left pane

Step 7- Choose Console Application in the middle pane.

Step 8- Enter the name of your project then click OK.

Step 9 – Right-click the project in Solution Explorer once the project is created

Step 10- Select Add

Step 11- Click References.

Step 12 – Select Assemblies

Step 13- Then click Extensions in the left pane and check Microsoft SharePoint in middle pane then click the Ok button.

Step 14- Right-click again the project in Solution Explorer and select Properties.

Step 15 – Click the Build tab in the left pane and uncheck the Prefer 32-bit option.

Conclusion

This book has successfully examined SharePoint development and the diverse ways to use the application for the best user experience. Here you can see how to create a site and effectively manage it alongside the structures of SharePoint which embodies folders and files. Being a guide to new users and also to enlighten those who already have acquaintance with SharePoint, this book is expected to guide users as they utilize the functionalities in SharePoint.

Printed in Great Britain
by Amazon